# SIMPLIFIED CSS3
# A Friendly Guide for
# Beginners

Master the Basics and Create Stunning Styles in Few
Steps

# Index

# Chapter 1: Introduction to CSS3

Web development has experienced constant evolution since its early days, and one of the fundamental pillars for styling web pages is CSS (Cascading Style Sheets). In this chapter, we dive into the fascinating world of CSS3, the latest version of the style sheet language that has revolutionized the way we design and present content on the web.

1.1 What is CSS?

CSS, or Cascading Style Sheets, is a style sheet language used to describe the presentation of a document written in HTML or XML. In other words, while HTML defines the structure and content of a web page, CSS is responsible for defining how that content is presented. This separation of responsibilities allows for greater flexibility and maintenance in web development.

With CSS, developers can specify style rules that dictate the appearance of specific elements or sets of elements on a web page. These rules include properties like color, font size, margins, spacing, and more. Additionally, CSS allows the creation of complex and responsive layouts through advanced techniques such as Flexbox and Grid.

1.2 Evolution of CSS: From CSS to CSS3

CSS has undergone several versions over time, and each new iteration has introduced significant features and improvements. The transition from CSS to CSS3 marked a major milestone in web development, introducing a number of advanced and modern features that allow developers to create richer and more engaging web experiences.

Some of the notable features of CSS3 include:

Transitions and Animations: CSS3 makes it easy to create smooth transition effects and animations without the need to use JavaScript.
Rounded Borders and Shadows: Properties like border-radius and box-shadow allow you to design elements with rounded corners and add shadows easily.

Gradients and Transparency: CSS3 allows the creation of color gradients and control of the opacity of elements, adding depth and style to web interfaces.
Media Queries: An essential feature for responsive design, which allows you to adapt the page style according to device characteristics, such as screen size.

1.3 Importance of CSS in Web Development

The importance of CSS in web development is undeniable. It not only allows for an attractive visual presentation, but also contributes to the usability and accessibility of a website. The ability to separate structure (HTML), presentation (CSS), and behavior (JavaScript) not only improves code readability, but also makes it easier to maintain and collaborate between development teams.

CSS3, in particular, has taken the web design experience to the next level by providing tools and techniques that were previously difficult to achieve without the use of additional images or scripts. The ability to create fluid animations, design flexible interfaces, and apply advanced styling has driven the evolution of web design and allowed developers to create visually stunning websites.

In summary, this chapter has given an overview of the importance of CSS in web development, from its beginnings to the most recent version, CSS3. In the following chapters, we dive deeper into CSS3-specific concepts and techniques so that newbies can build a solid foundation in effectively using this style sheet language. Let's continue exploring the exciting world of CSS3!

# Chapter 2: Basic Fundamentals - CSS Syntax

In the vast universe of web development, understanding CSS syntax is essential to building effective and attractive styles. This chapter will dive into the basics of CSS, providing newbies with a solid understanding of how to structure and apply style rules in their web projects.

2.1 CSS Syntax: The Basic Structure

Before we dive into the intricacies of style rules, it's crucial to understand the basic structure of CSS syntax. A style rule in CSS consists of a selector, a property, and a value, organized as follows:

```
selector {
  property: value;
}
```

Selector: Identifies the HTML elements to which the style rules will be applied. Can be the name of an element (such as p for paragraphs) or a class( .class) that has been assigned to one or more elements.

Property: Defines the specific feature that you want to stylize. It can be the color (color), the font size (font-size), the margins (margin), among other.
Value: Specifies the value to be assigned to the property. For example, for the color property, the value could be blue.

Let's look at a practical example:

```css
p {
  color: red;
  font-size: 16px;
  margin-bottom: 20px;
}
```

In this example, all <p> tags (paragraphs) will have a red text color, a font size of 16 pixels, and a bottom margin of 20 pixels.

2.2 Selectors and Attribute Selectors

Selectors are the backbone of style rules in CSS. They allow you to target specific elements or sets of elements on a web page. Below are some of the most common selectors:

Universal Selector (*): Selects all elements on the page.

Element Selector (element): Selects all elements of a specific type, such as p for paragraphs or h1 for level 1 headings.
Class Selector (.class): Selects all elements that have a specific class assigned, for example, .featured.

ID Selector (#id): Selects a unique element that has a specific identifier, for example, #header.

Attribute Selector ([attribute]): Selects elements that have a specific attribute, for example, [type] would select all elements with a type attribute.

Attribute selectors can be more specific, allowing you to select elements with specific attributes and values. For example:

```
input[type="text"] {
  border: 1px solid #ccc;
}
```

In this case, all <input> elements of type text will be selected and a solid light gray 1 pixel border will be applied to them.

2.3 Properties and Values

Properties and values in CSS are the building blocks for styling HTML elements. There are numerous properties ranging from box design to fonts and colors. Below are some common properties:

Color (color): Defines the color of the text. This can be a color name (such as red), a hexadecimal value (#FF0000), or an RGB value (rgb(255, 0, 0)).

Font Size (font-size): Sets the font size. It can be in pixels (px), ems (em) or percentages.

Margin (margin): Controls the space around an element. You can have values for each side (margin-top, margin-right, margin-bottom, margin-left).

Padding: Defines the space within an element. Like the margin, it can have values for each side.

These are just basic examples, but CSS offers a wide range of properties that allow detailed control over the appearance of HTML elements.

2.4 Box Model

The box model in CSS is essential to understanding how elements are represented and sized on a web page. Each HTML element is represented as a rectangular box, and the box model describes the properties that affect that box.
The key properties of the box model are:

Width and Height: Define the dimensions of the box.
Padding: Space between the contents of the box and its edge.

Edge (border): Exterior limit of the box. It can have properties such as thickness and style.
Margin (margin): Space between the edge of the box and the surrounding elements.

Understanding how these properties interact is essential to creating coherent and attractive designs. For example:

```
.my-box {
  width: 200px;
  height: 100px;
  padding: 10px;
  border: 2px solid #333;
  margin: 20px;
}
```

In this case, a box is created with a width of 200 pixels, a height of 100 pixels, a padding of 10 pixels, a solid border of 2 pixels, and a margin of 20 pixels around the box.

With these basics of syntax, selectors, properties, and the box model, novices will be well equipped to begin styling their web pages. In the following chapters, we'll dive even deeper into these ideas and explain advanced techniques to take web design skills to the next level. Let's keep building!

# Chapter 3: Text Style and Fonts

Text style and fonts play a crucial role in the visual presentation of a web page. In this chapter, we explore in depth the various CSS properties that allow you to format and customize text, as well as the options available for working with fonts. Understanding these tools is essential to achieving attractive and readable designs in any web project.

## 3.1 Text Properties

Text properties in CSS provide fine-grained control over the appearance and layout of textual content on a web page. Some of the most common properties are highlighted below:

Text Color (color): Defines the color of the text. It can be specified using a color name, a hexadecimal value, or RGB notation.

Font Size (font-size): Sets the size of the text. It can be expressed in pixels, ems, rem or percentages.

Letter-spacing: Controls the spacing between letters in the text.

Word-spacing: Defines the space between words.

Text Alignment (text-align): Controls the alignment of the text within its container, which can be left, right, centered or justified.

Text Decoration (text-decoration): Applies decorations such as underline, strikethrough, or none.

Text Transformation (text-transform): Modifies the capitalization style of the text, converting it to uppercase, lowercase or capitalizing each word.
Let's see a practical example of how to apply some of these properties:

```css
p {
  color: #333;
  font-size: 18px;
  letter-spacing: 1px;
  word-spacing: 2px;
  text-align: justify;
  text-decoration: underline;
  text-transform: uppercase;
}
```

In this case, all <p> elements (paragraphs) will have text with a dark color, font size of 18 pixels, letter and word spacing, justified alignment, underlining, and uppercase text.

3.2 Font Customization
Font choice is an integral part of web design, and CSS offers various properties to customize the appearance of fonts. Some of the key properties include:

Font Family (font-family): Defines the font used for the text. This can be a specific font, a list of supported fonts, or generic such as serif or sans-serif.

Font Style (font-style): Specifies the style of the font, such as normal, italic, or oblique.

Font-weight: Controls the weight of the font, such as light, normal, bold, or specific numbers.

Font Variants (font-variant): Allows you to adjust font characteristics, such as changing to lowercase or activating small letters.

Line Size (line-height): Defines the line height, which is the distance between lines of text. This can be a specific value or a multiple of the current font size.

An example of the application of these properties would be:

```
body {
  font-family: 'Arial', sans-serif;
  font-style: normal;
  font-weight: 400;
  font-variant: normal;
  font-size: 16px;
  line-height: 1.5;
}
```

Here, the body of the document (represented by body) will use the Arial font (or a falling sans-serif font), with normal style and weight, and a font size of 16 pixels, with a line height that is 1.5 times the font size.

3.3 Units of Measurement in CSS3

When working with text and font styles, it is crucial to understand the units of measurement available in CSS. Some of the most common units include:

Pixels (px): An absolute unit, specific to display devices such as screens and monitors.

Em (em): A relative unit based on the font size of the parent element. It is especially useful for making the design more flexible and adaptable.

Rem (rem): Similar to em, but is based on the font size of the root element (usually the <html>), providing global consistency throughout the document.

Percentages (%): A relative unit that refers to the size of the parent element.
Each unit has its place in web design, and choosing the right unit depends on the specific situation. For example, if a more flexible and scalable design is desired, em or rem units are preferable.

In summary, this chapter has thoroughly explored the fundamentals of text styling and fonts in CSS. By understanding text properties, customizing fonts, and choosing appropriate units of measurement, novice web developers will be well equipped to shape the textual presentation of their projects. In the following chapters, we dive into more advanced concepts, exploring techniques to achieve even more sophisticated and attractive designs. Let's continue advancing in the fascinating world of web development!

# Chapter 4: Layout Design and Colors

Visual design and the use of color are crucial aspects in web development, contributing significantly to the user experience. In this chapter, we will explain in detail how CSS3 facilitates layout design and how colors can be used effectively in a web project. Understanding these concepts is essential to creating attractive and coherent interfaces.

## 4.1 Backgrounds and Gradients

Backgrounds and gradients are essential tools to give life and depth to web interfaces. CSS3 offers versatile properties to handle backgrounds effectively. Some of the key properties include:

Background color (background-color): Defines the background color of an element. This can be a color name, hexadecimal value, or RGB notation.

Background Image (background-image): Allows you to set an image as the background of an element. This can be useful for achieving visual effects or design patterns.

Background Repetition (background-repeat): Controls how a background image is repeated, and can be repeated (repeat), not repeated (no-repeat), repeated only horizontally (repeat-x) or only vertically (repeat-y).
Background Position (background-position): Determines the initial position of a background image. You can use values like percentages or keywords like center or top.

Gradients (background-image with linear-gradient or radial-gradient): Allows you to create smooth transitions between two or more colors. Linear gradients follow a specific direction, while radial gradients expand from a central point.

An example of the application of these properties would be:

```
header {
  background-color: #2C3E50;
  color: #ECF0F1;
  padding: 20px;
  text-align: center;
    background-image: linear-gradient(to right, #3498db, #2c3e50);
}
```

In this case, the header will have a dark blue background (#2C3E50), a light text color (#ECF0F1), an internal padding of 20 pixels, centered text, and a background with a linear gradient that goes from a lighter shade to a darker shade of blue.

4.2 Embroidery and Borders

Embroidery and borders are key elements in layout design, helping to define and highlight specific areas of a web page. Border properties in CSS3 provide control over the style, thickness, and color of borders. Some of the properties include:

Border: Shorthand property that combines the border thickness, style, and color into a single value.

Border Thickness (border-width): Sets the thickness of the border. This can be a specific value in pixels (px), ems (em), or keywords such as thin, medium, or thin.

Border Style (border-style): Defines the style of the border, which can be solid, dotted, dashed, among others.

Border Color (border-color): Sets the border color. This can be a color name, hexadecimal value, or RGB notation.

Application example:

```
.thumbnail {
  border: 2px solid #3498db;
  padding: 10px;
  margin: 10px;
  border-radius: 5px;
}
```

In this example, elements with the .thumbnail class will have a solid 2 pixel blue border (#3498db), an inner padding of 10 pixels, a margin of 10 pixels, and rounded corners with a radius of 5 pixels.

4.3 Use of Colors in CSS3

The color palette in CSS3 is rich and varied, allowing a wide range of options to customize the visual appearance of a website. Some of the ways to define colors in CSS include:

Color Names (red, blue, etc.): CSS provides a set of predefined color names.

Hexadecimal Values (#RRGGBB): Specifies a color using a hexadecimal combination of the red, green, and blue components.

RGB Notation (rgb(r, g, b)): Allows you to define a color using the values of the red, green, and blue components in the range 0 to 255.

RGBA Notation (rgba(r, g, b, a)): Similar to RGB but with a fourth parameter (a) that represents the opacity of the color.

HSL (hsl(h, s%, l%)): Defines a color by its hue, saturation and luminosity.

HSLA (hsla(h, s%, l%, a)): Similar to HSL but with a fourth parameter (a) that represents opacity.

Application example:

```
.button {
  background-color: #27ae60;
  color: #fff;
  padding: 15px 20px;
  border: none;
  border-radius: 5px;
  cursor: pointer;
}
```

```
.button:hover {
  background-color: #2ecc71;
}
```

In this case, elements with the .button class will have a green background (#27ae60), white text (#fff), internal padding of 15 pixels vertically and 20 pixels horizontally, no border, rounded corners, and a change color when you hover over the button.

4.4 Transparency and Opacity

Transparency and opacity are powerful features that allow you to layer elements and create attractive visual effects. CSS3 offers two key properties to handle this:
Transparency (opacity): Defines the opacity of an element, where 0 is completely transparent and 1 is completely opaque.

RGBA (rgba(r, g, b, a)): Allows you to specify a color with a fourth parameter (a) that represents the opacity. This value ranges from 0 (transparent) to 1 (opaque).

Application example:

```
.modal {
  background-color: rgba(255, 255, 255, 0.9);
  border: 1px solid #ccc;
  padding: 20px;
  width: 300px;
  margin: 50px auto;
}
```

In this example, the element with the .modal class will have a white background with 90% opacity, a subtle border, internal padding, a fixed width of 300 pixels, and will be centered on the page.

4.5 Combining Design and Colors in Practical Projects

The effective combination of design and colors is evident in practical projects. Below is an example of how these concepts can be integrated to create an attractive image gallery:

```css
.gallery {
  display: flex;
  flex-wrap: wrap;
}

.gallery-item {
  flex: 1 0 300px;
  margin: 10px;
  overflow: hidden;
}

.gallery-item img {
  width: 100%;
  height: auto;
  transition: transform 0.3s ease-in-out;
}

.gallery-item:hover img {
```

```
  transform: scale(1.1);
}
```

In this example, the .gallery class uses flexible layout with Flexbox to create an image gallery. Each .gallery-item has a flexible width, a margin for separation, and the images within each item fit the width of the container. When you hover over an image, a scaling effect is applied to give dynamism to the interface.

4.6 Accessibility and Responsive Design Considerations

When designing and applying colors in a web project, it is crucial to consider accessibility and responsive design. Ensuring colors have enough contrast to be readable and considering the user experience on different devices are essential practices.

Contrast (color vs background-color): Ensuring that text and background have sufficient contrast to ensure readability, especially for those with visual impairments.

```
body {
  color: #333;
  background-color: #fff;
}
```

Responsive Design (media queries): Use media queries to adapt the design and colors according to the characteristics of the device.

```
@media screen and (max-width: 600px) {
```

```css
.sidebar {
  display: none;
}
}
```

These are just a few aspects of how layout and colors can be effectively integrated into web projects. In later chapters, we will explain more advanced and practical techniques to take your design and color palette to the next level. By applying these concepts, web developers can create attractive and functional interfaces that improve the user experience in their projects. Let's continue exploring the fascinating world of web design!

# Chapter 5: Responsive Design with CSS3

Responsive design has become an essential element in contemporary web development. In this chapter, we thoroughly explore CSS3 techniques and best practices for creating web interfaces that adapt fluidly to a variety of devices and screen sizes. Understanding and applying responsive design not only improves the user experience, but is also crucial to the performance and accessibility of a website.

5.1 Media Queries

Media Queries are the cornerstone of responsive design in CSS3. They allow you to apply specific styles based on device characteristics, such as screen width, orientation, pixel density, and more. Media Queries are commonly used to change the layout of a web page based on the screen size. Here is a basic example:

```
@media screen and (max-width: 600px) {
  body {
    font-size: 14px;
  }

  .sidebar {
    display: none;
  }
}
```

In this example, when the screen width is 600 pixels or less, a different style is applied to the document body and the .sidebar class. The font size is reduced and the sidebar is hidden, which is a common approach to accommodate smaller devices.

5.2 Fluid and Flexible Design

A fluid design is a key component of responsive design. It uses percentages instead of fixed values for the width of elements, allowing them to automatically adapt to the size of the container or screen. Flexbox and CSS Grid are powerful tools for creating flexible and fluid layouts.

```css
.container {
  display: flex;
  justify-content: space-between;
}


.column {
  flex: 1;
  margin: 10px;
}


@media screen and (max-width: 600px) {
  .container {
    flex-direction: column;
  }
}
```

In this example, the .container class uses Flexbox to layout its elements with space between them. When the screen width is 600 pixels or less, the flex direction is changed to column, rearranging elements vertically.

## 5.3 Adaptive Images

Images are a crucial component in any web design, and making them responsive is essential to ensure a consistent user experience across different devices. The max-width: 100% property is common practice to ensure that images do not exceed the width of the container and are automatically scaled.

```
img {
  max-width: 100%;
  height: auto;
}
```

This rule ensures that images are scaled proportionally and do not overflow from the parent container. This is especially important for devices with smaller screens where space is limited.

## 5.4 Flexbox for Responsive Design

Flexbox is a powerful and efficient tool for creating responsive designs. It allows the creation of flexible and adaptable structures without the need to float elements or use complicated margins and positioning.

```
.container {
  display: flex;
  justify-content: space-between;
}
```

```css
.item {
  flex: 1;
  margin: 10px;
}

@media screen and (max-width: 600px) {
  .container {
    flex-direction: column;
  }
}
```

In this example, the .container class uses Flexbox to layout its elements with space between them. When the screen width is 600 pixels or less, the flex direction is changed to column, providing a user experience more suitable for smaller devices.

5.5 Grid for Responsive Design

CSS Grid is another valuable tool for responsive design, allowing the creation of complex and structured layouts efficiently. It is especially useful for designing web pages with multiple sections and elements.

```css
.container {
  display: grid;
  grid-template-columns: repeat(3, 1fr);
  gap: 10px;
}
```

```css
@media screen and (max-width: 600px) {
.container {
  grid-template-columns: 1fr;
 }
}
```

In this example, the .container class uses Grid to define repeating columns of equal size. When the screen width is 600 pixels or less, it changes to a single column, making it easier to view on smaller devices.

5.6 Relative Units and Responsive Design

Using relative units, such as ems and rems, is essential for responsive design. Unlike absolute units like pixels, relative units scale proportionally to the size of the parent element, making it easier to create flexible layouts.

```css
body {
  font-size: 16px;
}
h1 {
  font-size: 2em; /* 32px */
}
```

```css
@media screen and (max-width: 600px) {
  body {
    font-size: 14px;
 }
}
```

In this example, the document body font size is set to 16 pixels, and the headings (h1) font size is set to 2in, resulting in a font size of 32 pixels. When the screen width is 600 pixels or less, the font size of the document body is set to 14 pixels, which automatically affects the font size of the headers.

5.7 Responsive Design and Accessibility

Accessibility is an integral component of responsive design. Ensuring that a website is accessible to all users, regardless of ability or device, is essential. Here are some key practices:

Color Contrast: Ensure there is sufficient contrast between the text and the background to improve readability.

```
body {
  color: #333;
  background-color: #fff;
}
```

Using Relative Font Sizes: Use relative font sizes, such as ems or rems, to allow users to adjust the text size to their preferences.

```
body {
  font-size: 16px;
}
```

```
@media screen and (max-width: 600px) {
```

```
body {
  font-size: 14px;
}
}
```

Descriptive Images: Provide alternative descriptions (alt attribute) for all images so that visually impaired users can understand the image content.

```
<img src="image.jpg" alt="Image description">
```
Logical Reading Order: Ensure that the reading order of content is logical and semantic, which benefits users who use assistive technologies such as screen readers.

```
<none>
<ul>
  <li><a href="#">Start</a></li>
  <li><a href="#">About</a></li>
  <li><a href="#">Contact</a></li>
</ul>
</none>
```

User Testing: Conduct testing with users with disabilities to identify potential accessibility issues and make continuous improvements.

Responsive design and accessibility must go hand in hand to ensure that everyone, regardless of their abilities or devices, can fully access and enjoy the web experience.

5.8 Advanced Techniques for Responsive Design

In addition to the basic techniques, there are several advanced techniques that can take responsive design to a higher level:

WebP Images: Use the WebP format for images, as it offers superior compression without compromising quality, improving performance on mobile devices.

```css
/* Using media query to load WebP images in supported browsers */
@media (min-width: 600px) {
  .image {
    background: url('imagen.webp') center/cover;
  }
}
/* Load JPEG images for browsers that do not support WebP */
@supports (background: url('imagen.webp')) {
  .image {
    background: url('image.jpg') center/cover;
  }
}
```

Lazy Loading Images: Delay loading images that are not in the visible part of the page until the user scrolls to them.

```html
<img data-src="image.jpg" alt="Image description">
<script>
  document.addEventListener('DOMContentLoaded', function()
{
    var lazyImages =
[].slice.call(document.querySelectorAll('img[data-src]'));
```

```
    if ('IntersectionObserver' in window) {
        var lazyImageObserver = new
IntersectionObserver(function(entries, observer) {
            entries.forEach(function(entry) {
                if (entry.isIntersecting) {
                    waslazyImage = entry.target;
                    lazyImage.src = lazyImage.dataset.src;
                    lazyImageObserver.unobserve(lazyImage);
                }
            });
        });

        lazyImages.forEach(function(lazyImage) {
            lazyImageObserver.observe(lazyImage);
        });
    }
});
</script>
```

Content-Based Design: Use techniques such as Flexible Display Unit (VW) to base the size of some elements on the width of the viewport, ensuring a consistent visual experience.

```
h1 {
    font-size: 5vw;
}
```

These advanced techniques can further improve performance and user experience on devices with different capabilities and screen sizes.

5.9 Tools and Resources for Responsive Design

Various tools and resources are available to facilitate and optimize the responsive design process. Some of them include:

Viewport Resizer: A browser extension that allows you to preview a website on various screen sizes.

Responsive Design Mode in Browsers: Development tools in modern browsers offer responsive modes that make it easy to simulate mobile devices and adjust the design in real time.
CSS Frameworks: Use CSS frameworks such as Bootstrap or Foundation, which provide predefined components and styles to facilitate the creation of responsive designs.

Media Query Generators: Online tools that automatically generate media queries based on the needs of responsive design.

Google PageSpeed Insights: Evaluate the performance of a website and receive suggestions to optimize it, including improvements to responsive design.

5.10 Conclusions and Look to the Future

Responsive design has evolved from being an option to becoming a standard in web development. As the diversity of devices and screen sizes continues to expand, responsive design will continue to be essential to ensure a consistent and engaging user experience.

It is crucial that web developers understand responsive design best practices and are aware of the latest technologies and tools that facilitate effective implementation. Accessibility and performance should remain critical considerations when designing responsive interfaces, and extensive testing on a variety of devices is key to ensuring the effectiveness of responsive design.

As we move into the future of web development, new technologies and approaches are likely to emerge to further improve the flexibility and efficiency of responsive design. Staying up to date with web design trends and evolving technologies is essential to delivering exceptional experiences on the web of tomorrow.

In conclusion, responsive design is not only a web development technique, but an essential approach to ensuring that websites are accessible and functional on the diversity of devices that users use today. By applying the techniques and best practices described in this chapter, web developers can create engaging and consistent user experiences on any screen. Let's keep moving forward in the exciting world of responsive design and web development!

# Chapter 6: Transformations and Transitions in CSS3

Transforms and transitions in CSS3 offer web developers powerful tools to add dynamism and elegance to interfaces. In this chapter, we will explain in detail the transformation and transition properties, how to apply them effectively, and how they can improve the user experience in modern web development.

## 6.1 Transformations in CSS3

Transformations in CSS3 allow you to modify the visual appearance of elements by manipulating properties such as rotation, scale, translation and skew. These transformations provide an efficient way to create attractive visual effects without the need to use additional images or complex scripts.

### 6.1.1 transform property

The transform property is the cornerstone of transformations in CSS3. It can be applied to any HTML element and offers a variety of functions to modify its visual presentation. Some of the most common transformations include:

rotate(angle): Rotates the element clockwise by the specified angle.

```
.box {
  transform: rotate(45deg);
```

```
}
```

scale(x, y): Scales the element horizontally (x) and vertically (y). A value of 1 means no change, while higher or lower values will change the scale.

```
.box {
  transform: scale(1.5, 0.8);
}
```

translate(x, y): Translates the element on the horizontal (x) and vertical (y) axis. Values can be pixels, percentages, or relative units.

```
.box {
  transform: translate(20px, -10px);
}
```

skew(x, y): Applies a skew to the element on the horizontal (x) and vertical (y) axis. The values represent angles.

```
.box {
  transform: skew(10deg, -5deg);
}
```

These transformations can be combined to achieve more complex and creative effects. For example, to rotate and scale simultaneously:

```
.box {
```

```css
  transform: rotate(45deg) scale(1.2, 1.2);
}
```

## 6.1.2 3D Transformations

CSS3 also allows transformations to be performed in three dimensions, which adds an extra dimension to standard transformations. This provides the possibility of creating more realistic and complex effects.

rotateX(angle), rotateY(angle), rotateZ(angle): Rotate the element around the X, Y and Z axes, respectively.

```css
.box {
  transform: rotateX(45deg) rotateY(30deg) rotateZ(15deg);
}
```
scale3d(x, y, z): Scales the element in all three dimensions.
```css
.box {
  transform: scale3d(1.5, 0.8, 2);
}
```
translate3d(x, y, z): Translates the element in all three dimensions.
css
Copy code
```css
.box {
  transform: translate3d(20px, -10px, 30px);
}
```

These 3D transformations open new possibilities for creating immersive and engaging visual experiences in web development.

6.1.3 Transformation Origin

The transformed property origin allows you to specify the point around which the transformations are applied. By default, this point is the center of the element, but it can be adjusted according to the needs of the design.

```
.box {
  transform-origin: top left;
}
```

In this example, the transformation will be applied around the top left corner of the element instead of its center.

6.2 Transitions in CSS3

Transitions in CSS3 allow you to smooth the state changes of an element over a specified time interval. By defining the properties to animate and the duration of the transition, developers can improve the user experience by providing more pleasing and natural visual changes.

6.2.1 Transition property
The transition property is used to specify transitions from one state to another. It is made up of four main values: the property that it will transition, the duration of the transition, the timing function and an optional delay.

```
.box {
```

```
transition: transform 0.5s ease-in-out 0.2s;
}
```

In this example, the transform property will transition in 0.5 seconds, using a timing function that starts slowly, speeds up in the middle, and then slows down again, with a 0.2 second delay before the transition begins.

6.2.2 Timing Functions

Timing functions define how the interpolation is performed between the initial and final states of the transition. Some common features include:

ease: Start slowly, speed up in the middle, and then slow down at the end.

linear: Performs the transition at a constant speed.
ease-in: Start slowly and speed up towards the end.

ease-out: Starts quickly and slows down towards the end.

ease-in-out: Start slowly, speed up in the middle, then slow down at the end.

These features allow you to adapt the feel of the transition according to the needs of the design.

6.2.3 Multiple Transitions

The transition property also allows the specification of multiple properties and their respective transition settings.

```
.box {
  transition: transform 0.5s ease-in-out, opacity 0.3s linear;
}
```

In this example, both the transform property and the opacity They will have separate transition settings.

6.2.4 Transition Events

JavaScript can be used to detect transition events, allowing specific actions to be taken in response to state changes. The most common events include transitionstart, transitionend ytransitioncancel.

```
const box = document.querySelector('.box');

box.addEventListener('transitionend', () => {
  console.log('The transition has ended.');
});
```

In this example, a message will be printed to the console when the checkout transition completes.

6.3 Integrating Transformations and Transitions into Practical Projects

The true power of transformations and transitions in CSS3 is revealed when they are integrated into practical projects. Below is an example of how these properties can be used to improve the user experience in an image gallery:

```
<!DOCTYPE html>

<html lang="es">
```

```html
<head>
  <meta charset="UTF-8">
    <meta   name="viewport"   content="width=device-width,
initial-scale=1.0">
  <title>Image Gallery</title>
  <style>
  .gallery {
    display: flex;
    flex-wrap: wrap;
  }
  .gallery-item {
    flex: 1 0 300px;
    margin: 10px;
    overflow: hidden;
    transition: transform 0.3s ease-in-out;
  }

  .gallery-item img {
    width: 100%;
    height: auto;
  }

  .gallery-item:hover {
    transform: scale(1.1);
  }
  </style>
</head>
<body>
```

```
<div class="gallery">
  <div class="gallery-item">
    <img src="image1.jpg" alt="Image 1">
  </div>
  <div class="gallery-item">
    <img src="image2.jpg" alt="Image 2">
  </div>
  <div class="gallery-item">
    <img src="image3.jpg" alt="Image 3">
  </div>
  <!-- Add more elements as needed -->
</div>
</body>
</html>
```

In this example, the image gallery uses transforms to apply a scaling effect when the user hovers over an image. The smooth transition provides a pleasant visual experience, and integrating these properties into the project flow is simple and effective.

6.4 Considerations and Good Practices

When working with transformations and transitions, it is essential to consider some best practices to ensure optimal performance and a positive user experience:

Minimize the Use of Transitions in Complex Design Elements: In elements with a large amount of content or complex design, excessive use of transitions can affect performance. It is important to evaluate and optimize as necessary.

Apply Transitions to Properties That Can Be Hardware Accelerated: Properties like transform and opacity are typically hardware accelerated, meaning they are handled more efficiently to deliver smoother performance.

Use Meaningful Transitions: Transitions should have a purpose and improve the user experience. Avoid excessive or unnecessary use of transitions so as not to distract the user.

Consider accessibility: When applying transformations, especially those that affect visual design, it is essential to consider accessibility. Ensure that transformations do not negatively impact the readability of content or make interaction difficult for users with disabilities.

Testing on Multiple Browsers and Devices: Transforms and transitions may behave differently on various browsers and devices. Extensive testing is crucial to ensure consistency and proper operation across the spectrum.

6.5 Tools and Resources for Transformations and Transitions

To facilitate the implementation and optimization of transformations and transitions, there are several tools and resources available:

Can I Use (caniuse.com): An online resource that provides information on cross-browser compatibility of CSS properties.

CSS3 Transitions and Transforms Cheat Sheet: Cheat sheets summarizing the properties and values available for transformations and transitions in CSS3.

Animista (animista.net): An online tool that allows you to generate CSS code for a variety of predefined animations and transitions.

GreenSock Animation Platform (GSAP): A JavaScript library that makes it easy to create advanced animations, including transformations and transitions, with superior performance.

## 6.6 Conclusions and Future Perspectives

Transforms and transitions in CSS3 have revolutionized the way web developers can add dynamism and style to their projects. From simple hover effects to complex animations, these properties offer versatility and creativity.

As the web evolves, we're likely to see even more advancements in animations and transitions, with the ability to integrate emerging technologies like the Web Animations API for greater control and performance. Combining transformations and transitions with other technologies, such as SVG and WebGL, will also open up new opportunities for amazing visual experiences.

Ultimately, the key to making the most of these properties lies in practice and experimentation. By effectively integrating transformations and transitions into practical projects, web developers can elevate the quality and interactivity of their sites, providing more engaging and immersive online experiences.

# Chapter 7: Layout and Flexbox Design in CSS3

The layout design and Flexbox property in CSS3 have radically transformed the way web developers approach the structure and design of user interfaces. This chapter explores these fundamental tools in detail, from the basic concepts to their practical application in web projects. As we delve deeper into the world of layout design and Flexbox, we'll discover how these technologies have simplified the creation of flexible and responsive layouts.

## 7.1 Introduction to Layout Design in CSS3

Layout layout, also known as grid layout, is a modern approach to creating web designs. Provides a more efficient and predictable structure for organizing and aligning content on a page. With layout design, web developers can divide the interface into rows and columns, creating a grid that makes it easy to arrange and align elements.

### 7.1.1 Layout Design Properties

Key properties of the layout design include:

display: grid;: Sets a container as a grid.

```
.container {
  display: grid;
  grid-template-columns: repeat(3, 1fr);
  grid-gap: 20px;
}
```

In this example, the container is defined as a grid with three columns of equal size and a space of 20 pixels between them.

grid-template-columns and grid-template-rows: Define the size and arrangement of columns and rows in the grid.

```
.container {
  grid-template-columns: 100px 200px auto;
  grid-template-rows: 50px auto;
}
```

Here, you specify a grid with three columns of fixed sizes and two rows, one with a fixed size and one that takes up the remaining space.

grid-column and grid-row: Control which columns and rows elements are placed in.

```
.item {
  grid-column: 2 / 4;
  grid-row: 1 / 3;
}
```

This example positions an element in columns 2 through 4 and rows 1 through 3 of the grid.

grid-gap: Defines the space between the rows and columns of the grid.

```
.container {
```

```
  grid-gap: 10px;
}
```

In this case, a space of 10 pixels is set between all rows and columns of the grid.

7.1.2 Creating Flexible and Responsive Layouts with Layout Design

Layout design is especially powerful when it comes to creating flexible and responsive layouts. It can easily adapt to different screen sizes and devices by using relative units and media queries.

```
.container {
  display: grid;
  grid-template-columns: repeat(auto-fit, minmax(200px, 1fr));
  grid-gap: 20px;
}
```
In this example, the grid-template-columns property uses the repeat function along with auto-fit to create as many columns as possible that have a minimum width of 200 pixels and are expandan depending on available space. This allows the layout to dynamically adjust to smaller screens without sacrificing readability or aesthetics.

7.2 Going deeper into Flexbox in CSS3

Flexbox, or Flexible Box Layout, is a layout technique that simplifies creating complex layouts and aligning elements in a single dimension, either horizontal or vertical. Flexbox is especially useful for creating smaller interfaces and individual components.

7.2.1 Flexbox Basics

display: flex;: Converts a container to a flexible container.

```
.container {
  display: flex;
}
```

In this case, all direct children of .container become flex elements.

flex-direction: Defines the main address of the flex container.

```
.container {
  flex-direction: row; /* Default value */
  /* Can also be column, row-reverse or column-reverse */
}
```

This example sets the main direction of the flex container to horizontal (left to right).

justify-content: Align flex elements along the main axis.

```
.container {
    justify-content: space-between; /* También puede ser
flex-start, flex-end, center, space-around o space-evenly */
}
```

Here, the elements are distributed evenly along the main axis with a gap between them.
align-items: Aligns flex items along the secondary axis.

```
.container {
    align-items: center; /* Can also be flex-start, flex-end,
stretch, baseline or safe/stretch (in some cases) */
}
```

This example aligns the elements vertically in the center of the flex container.

7.2.2 Advanced Flexbox Properties

flex: Combines the flex-grow, flex-shrink, and flex-basis properties into a single property.

```
.item {
  flex: 1 0 200px;
}
```

Here, the element will expand to take up any extra space available, will not collapse, and has a base size of 200 pixels.
align-self: Overrides the default alignment defined by align-items for a specific item.

```
.item {
  align-self: flex-end; /* Can also be flex-start, center, baseline
or stretch */
}
```

This example aligns a specific element to the bottom end of the secondary axis.

### 7.2.3 Responsive Design with Flexbox

Flexbox is especially useful for responsive design due to its ability to adapt to different screen sizes and content layouts. When combined with media queries, it allows you to create interfaces that adapt effectively to diverse devices.

```css
.container {
  display: flex;
  flex-direction: column; /* Switch to column on smaller screens */
}
.item {
  flex: 1;
}
```

In this case, the main direction of the flex container is changed to column on smaller screens, making it easier to adapt the layout.

### 7.3 Integrating Layout Design and Flexbox into Practical Projects

The true power of layout design and Flexbox comes through when applied in practical projects. Below is a simple example of how these properties can be used to create a flexible and responsive navigation bar:

```html
<!DOCTYPE html>
<html lang="es">
<head>
 <meta charset="UTF-8">
 <meta name="viewport" content="width=device-width,
initial-scale=1.0">
 <title>Navigation Bar</title>
 <style>
  are not {
    display: flex;
    justify-content: space-between;
    align-items: center;
    padding: 20px;
    background-color: #333;
    color: #fff;
  }

  ul {
    list-style: none;
    display: flex;
  }

  that {
    margin-right: 20px;
  }

  @media (max-width: 600px) {
    are not {
```

```
    flex-direction: column;
    align-items: flex-start;
  }


  ul {
    margin-top: 10px;
  }
}
</style>
</head>
<body>
<none>
 <h1>Logo</h1>
 <ul>
   <li><a href="#">Start</a></li>
   <li><a href="#">About</a></li>
   <li><a href="#">Contact</a></li>
 </ul>
</none>
</body>
</html>
```

In this example, the navigation bar uses Flexbox to align content horizontally and adjusts to a vertical layout on smaller screens. Easily applying these properties significantly improves readability and user experience across devices.

7.4 Considerations and Good Practices

When working with layout design and Flexbox, it is crucial to keep a few considerations in mind and follow good practices to ensure effectiveness and consistency in web design:

Combine Layout Design and Flexbox as needed: Both techniques can be used together to take advantage of their respective strengths. For example, you can use layout layout for the overall structure and Flexbox to align elements within those areas.

Consider Browser Compatibility: Although layout and Flexbox support is extensive in modern browsers, it is always advisable to check compatibility at Can I Use (caniuse.com) and provide fallback solutions if necessary.

Avoid Excessive Use of Nesting: While layout and Flexbox layout allow nesting of elements, it is crucial to avoid excessive nesting to keep the code clean and easy to understand. Use layout and Flexbox layout properties on the appropriate elements without unnecessary nesting.

Think in Responsive Design Terms: Both technologies are fundamental to responsive design, and their use should align with the overall vision of providing a consistent experience across devices of different sizes.

7.5 Tools and Resources for Layout and Flexbox Design

Numerous tools and resources are available to facilitate the implementation and optimization of layout and Flexbox design in web projects:

Grid by Example (gridbyexample.com): An excellent source of tutorials and practical examples for learning layout design.

Flexbox Froggy (flexboxfroggy.com): An interactive game that teaches Flexbox in a fun and hands-on way.

CSS Grid Generator (cssgrid-generator.netlify.app): An online tool that allows you to generate custom layout design code visually.

Flexbox Patterns (flexboxpatterns.com): A collection of common design patterns created with Flexbox.

Can I Use (caniuse.com): An online resource for checking browser compatibility with web properties and technologies, including layout design and Flexbox.

7.6 Conclusions and Future Perspectives

Layout and Flexbox design in CSS3 have revolutionized the way web developers approach creating flexible and responsive layouts. From simplifying structure to efficiently aligning elements, these technologies have paved the way for more attractive and functional user interfaces.

As we advance in web development, we are likely to see continued improvements in layout design and Flexbox, as well as the emergence of new technologies that complement and expand their capabilities. Combining these tools with other emerging technologies, such as

CSS Grid and CSS Variables, will open up new possibilities for creating innovative web designs.

In conclusion, layout design and Flexbox are not only essential tools for modern web developers, but also the foundation of effective and responsive web designs. By making the most of these technologies and staying up to date with best practices and new trends.

# Chapter 8: Layout and Grid Design in CSS3

The layout design and Grid property in CSS3 have transformed the way web developers approach creating complex and flexible layouts. This chapter explores these tools in depth, from the basic concepts to their practical application in web projects.

8.1 Introduction to Layout Design in CSS3

Layout layout, also known as grid layout, provides a powerful approach to creating web designs. It is based on the creation of a flexible grid that organizes elements in rows and columns, allowing precise control of the page layout.

8.1.1 Main Properties of the Layout Design

display: grid;: This property sets a container as a grid container.

```
.container {
  display: grid;
```

```
  grid-template-columns: repeat(3, 1fr);
  grid-gap: 20px;
}
```

Here, the container becomes a grid with three columns of equal size and a space of 20 pixels between them.

grid-template-columns and grid-template-rows: These properties define the size and layout of the columns and rows in the grid.

```
.container {
  grid-template-columns: 100px 200px auto;
  grid-template-rows: 50px auto;
}
```

This example specifies a grid with three columns of fixed sizes and two rows, one with a fixed size and one that takes up the remaining space.

grid-column and grid-row: These properties control which columns and rows elements are placed in.

```
.item {
  grid-column: 2 / 4;
  grid-row: 1 / 3;
}
```

In this case, the element is positioned in columns 2 to 4 and rows 1 to 3 of the grid.

grid-gap: This property defines the space between the rows and columns of the grid.

```
.container {
  grid-gap: 10px;
}
```

Here, a space of 10 pixels is set between all rows and columns of the grid.

8.1.2 Creating Flexible and Responsive Layouts with Layout Design

Layout design is especially powerful when it comes to creating flexible and responsive layouts. It can easily adapt to different screen sizes and devices by using relative units and media queries.

```
.container {
  display: grid;
  grid-template-columns: repeat(auto-fit, minmax(200px, 1fr));
  grid-gap: 20px;
}
```

In this example, the grid-template-columns property uses the repeat function along with auto-fit to create as many columns as possible that have a minimum width of 200 pixels and are expandan depending on available space. This allows the layout to dynamically adjust to smaller screens without sacrificing readability or aesthetics.

8.2 Delving into the Grid Property in CSS3

The Grid property provides a two-dimensional grid system that goes beyond the capabilities of the layout layout. Allows you to divide the layout into rows and columns, providing more detailed control over the layout and layout of elements.

8.2.1 Basic Principles of Grid Property

display: grid;: This property converts a container to a grid container.

```
.container {
  display: grid;
}
```

With this declaration, all direct child elements of .container become grid elements.

grid-template-areas: This property assigns names to specific areas of the grid, allowing for more semantic layout.

```
.container {
  grid-template-areas:
    'header header header'
    'sidebar main main'
    'footer footer footer';
}
```

Here, areas are defined for the header, sidebar, main content, and footer.

grid-area: This property assigns an element to a specific area of the grid defined by grid-template.areas.

```
.header {
  grid-area: header;
}

.sidebar {
  grid-area: sidebar;
}

.main {
  grid-area: main;
}

.footer {
  grid-area: footer;
}
```

This assigns each element to its corresponding area on the grid.

8.2.2 Advanced Properties of the Grid Property

grid-template-columns and grid-template-rows: These properties define the size and layout of the columns and rows in the grid.

```
.container {
  grid-template-columns: 1fr 2fr 1fr;
```

```
  grid-template-rows: 100px auto 50px;
}
```

In this example, three columns with the specified relative width and three rows with specific heights are created.

grid-column and grid-row: These properties control which columns and rows elements are placed in.

```
.item {
  grid-column: 2 / 4;
  grid-row: 1 / 3;
}
```

Here, the element is positioned in columns 2 to 4 and rows 1 to 3 of the grid.

grid-gap: This property defines the space between the rows and columns of the grid.

```
.container {
  grid-gap: 10px;
}
```

In this case, a space of 10 pixels is set between all rows and columns of the grid.

8.2.3 Creating Complex Layouts with the Grid Property

The Grid property allows the creation of complex layouts by combining the properties mentioned above. For example, a blog layout could be structured as follows:

```css
.container {
  display: grid;
  grid-template-columns: 1fr 3fr;
  grid-template-areas:
    'header header'
    'sidebar main'
    'footer footer';
}

.header {
  grid-area: header;
}

.sidebar {
  grid-area: sidebar;
}

.main {
  grid-area: main;
}

.footer {
  grid-area: footer;
}
```

In this case, the grid container is divided into three main areas: header, sidebar, main content, and footer. Each section occupies a specific part of the grid, providing an organized and easy-to-maintain layout.

## 8.3 Integrating Layout and Grid Design into Practical Projects

The true power of layout and Grid design comes through when applied in practical projects. Below is an example of how these properties can be used to create a web portfolio layout:

```html
<!DOCTYPE html>
<html lang="es">
<head>
  <meta charset="UTF-8">
  <meta name="viewport" content="width=device-width,
initial-scale=1.0">
  <title>Portafolio</title>
  <style>
    body {
      font-family: 'Arial', sans-serif;
      margin: 0;
      padding: 0;
    }

    header {
      background-color: #333;
      color: #fff;
      padding: 20px;
      text-align: center;
    }
```

```css
  are not {
    display: grid;
    grid-template-columns: repeat(4, 1fr);
    background-color: #555;
    padding: 10px;
  }

  section {
    display: grid;
    grid-template-columns: repeat(auto-fill, minmax(250px,
1fr));
    grid-gap: 20px;
    padding: 20px;
  }

  article {
    border: 1px solid #ddd;
    padding: 10px;
    text-align: center;
  }

  footer {
    background-color: #333;
    color: #fff;
    padding: 10px;
    text-align: center;
  }
</style>
```

```html
</head>
<body>
 <header>
   <h1>Portfolio</h1>
 </header>

 <none>
  <a href="#">Start</a>
  <a href="#">Projects</a>
  <a href="#">About</a>
  <a href="#">Contact</a>
 </none>

 <section>
   <article>Project 1</article>
   <article>Project 2</article>
   <article>Project 3</article>
   <!-- Add more projects as needed -->
 </section>

 <footer>
   <p>&copy; 2023 Portfolio. All rights reserved.</p>
 </footer>
</body>
</html>
```

In this example, both the layout layout and the Grid property are used to create a simple but effective web page layout. The header and footer are set to the layout layout, while the navigation bar and projects section use the Grid property to organize and align elements efficiently.

## 8.4 Considerations and Good Practices

When working with layout and Grid design, it is important to keep some considerations in mind and follow good practices to ensure an efficient design and user experience.

Grid Planning: Before implementing a layout layout or grid, it is essential to plan the grid structure and allocate specific areas for different sections of the layout.

Responsive Use: Both technologies are highly compatible with responsive design. It is crucial to use relative units and media queries to ensure that the layout adapts effectively to different screen sizes.

Browser Compatibility: Although layout and Grid layout support is extensive in modern browsers, it is always advisable to check compatibility at Can I Use (caniuse.com) and provide backup solutions if necessary.

Experimentation with Fractions andAuto-Fit: When experimenting with the Grid property, the combination of fractions (fr) andauto-fit can provide a flexible and easily adaptable design.

Reusing Classes and Components: When creating complex designs, it is useful to reuse classes and components to keep the code clean and modular.

## 8.5 Tools and Resources for Layout and Grid Design

Numerous tools and resources are available to facilitate the implementation and optimization of layout and Grid design in web projects:

CSS Grid Generator (cssgrid-generator.netlify.app): An online tool that allows you to generate custom grid code visually.

Grid by Example (gridbyexample.com): A valuable source of tutorials and practical examples to learn and master the Grid property.

Can I Use (caniuse.com): An online resource for checking browser compatibility with web properties and technologies, including layout design and Grid.

8.6 Conclusions and Future Perspectives

The layout layout and Grid property in CSS3 have revolutionized the way web developers create and structure complex layouts. From grid simplification to the ability to create responsive and adaptive layouts, these technologies have taken web design to a new level.

As we continue to advance web development, we are likely to see continued improvements in layout and Grid design, as well as the addition of new features and capabilities. Combining these tools with other emerging technologies, such as Flexbox and CSS Variables, will continue to drive the creation of innovative user interfaces.

In short, layout and Grid design are not only essential tools for modern web developers, but also the backbone of web designs.staff and adaptable. By making the most of these technologies and staying up-to-date with best practices and new trends, developers can continue to provide exceptional experiences on the web of the future. Let's continue exploring and experimenting in the exciting world of layout design and Grid in web development!

# Chapter 9: Optimization and Practices in Web Development

Optimization and the implementation of good practices are essential in today's web development. This chapter will delve into various aspects related to optimizing performance, accessibility, security, and other essential practices that ensure the creation of efficient and sustainable websites.

## 9.1 Performance Optimization

Performance optimization is a critical aspect of web development as it directly affects the user experience and application efficiency. Here, we will explain some strategies and best practices to improve website performance.

### 9.1.1 Efficient Resource Loading

Minification of CSS and JavaScript Files: Minification involves removing whitespace, comments, and reducing variable names to reduce the size of CSS and JavaScript files. Use tools like UglifyJS and Terser for JavaScript, and cssnano for CSS, can help achieve this process automatically.

```
# Minification example with Terser for JavaScript
terser script.js -o script.min.js
```

Image Compression: Images are often responsible for a significant portion of the page size. Using efficient image formats like WebP and image compression tools like ImageOptim or TinyPNG can dramatically reduce image size without compromising visual quality.

Asynchronous and Lazy Loading of Resources: Using the async or defer property when including JavaScript files allows the loading of the page to not be hindered by the execution of scripts. This improves the initial loading speed.

```html
<!-- Asynchronous loading -->
<script async src="script.js"></script>
```

```html
<!-- Lazy loading -->
<script defer src="script.js"></script>
```

### 9.1.2 Efficient Use of Caches

Client- and Server-Side Caching: Leveraging browser caching for static resources and setting cache headers on the server can reduce the number of requests to the server and speed up page loading on subsequent visits.

```nginx
# Cache configuration in Nginx
location ~* \.(jpg|jpeg|png|gif|ico|css|js)$ {
    expires 30d;
    add_header Cache-Control "public, max-age=2592000";
}
```

### 9.1.3 Reduction in the Number of Requests

File Bundling: Combine CSS and JavaScript files into single files to reduce the number of requests to the server. Tools like Webpack and Parcel can automate this process.

Using Image Sprites: Combine multiple images into a single sprite to reduce requests for individual images.

## 9.2 Accessibility and Good Practice in Design

Accessibility is an essential aspect of web design, and ensuring that a site is accessible to all people, regardless of their abilities or disabilities, is a fundamental responsibility of the developer.

### 9.2.1 HTML Semantics

Proper Use of HTML Tags: Using semantic and meaningful HTML tags not only improves accessibility, but also helps search engines understand the structure of the content.

```
<!-- Use of semantic tags -->
<article>
  <h2>Article Title</h2>
  <p>Article Content...</p>
</article>
```

### 9.2.2 ARIA (Accessible Rich Internet Applications)

Using ARIA Attributes: ARIA provides additional attributes that can add semantic information and improve the accessibility of interactive elements, such as drop-down menus and modal dialogs.

```
<!-- Example of ARIA attributes for a dropdown menu -->
<button    aria-haspopup="true"    aria-controls="menu1"
id="button1">Open Menu</button>
<ul id="menu1" role="menu" aria-labelledby="button1">
  <!-- Menu contents -->
</ul>
```

## 9.2.3 Navigation and Keyboard

Logical Navigation: Ensure site navigation is logical and sequential, making it easy for users to understand and navigate with assistive devices.
Focusability and Keyboard Accessibility: Ensure that all site functions are accessible and usable via keyboard. This benefits people with visual or motor disabilities.

```
/* Make focusable elements visible when receiving keyboard
focus */
:focus {
  outline: 2px solid #4d90fe;
}
```

## 9.3 Security in Web Development

Security is a crucial aspect of web development, and adopting good practices from the beginning is essential to protect websites against threats and vulnerabilities.

## 9.3.1 Protection against Common Attacks

Server-Side Validation: Always validate data server-side to prevent injection attacks and ensure data is secure before processing.

```php
// PHP validation example
$username = $_POST['username'];
if (preg_match('/^[a-zA-Z0-9_]{5,20}$/', $username)) {
 // Process the username
} else {
 // Invalid username
  echo "Invalid username";
}
```

User Data Escaping: When displaying user-supplied data in the user interface, be sure to escape the data to prevent scripting attacks.

```javascript
// Escape example in JavaScript
function escapeHTML(text) {
  var div = document.createElement('div');
  div.innerText = text;
   return div.innerHTML;
}
```

9.3.2 Session Management and Authentication

Use of Secure Tokens: When implementing authentication, use secure tokens and practices such as JWT (JSON Web Tokens) to ensure the integrity and authenticity of information transmitted between the client and the server.

Secure Logout: Implement secure logout to ensure that the user's session is properly logged out and that no active session tokens remain after disconnection.

```php
// Example of logout in PHP
session_start();
session_destroy();
```

### 9.3.3 Update and Maintenance

Regular Update of Dependencies: Keep dependencies up to date, including libraries, frameworks, and operating systems, to mitigate known vulnerabilities.

```
# Updating dependencies in Node.js
npm update
```

Security Audit: Conduct regular security audits to identify and address potential vulnerabilities in code and infrastructure.

## 9.4 Testing and Automation

Automation and testing are essential components to ensure code quality and stability in web development. Continuous integration (CI) and continuous delivery (CD) are key practices in this area.

### 9.4.1 Unit and Integration Tests

Jasmine and Mocha for Unit Testing: Use testing libraries such as Jasmine or Mocha to perform unit tests that evaluate the individual functioning of functions and components.

```
// Example of unit testing with Jasmine
describe('Sum Function', function() {
  it('should add two numbers correctly', function() {
    expect(sum(2, 3)).toBe(5);
  });
});
```

Integration Testing with Selenium: Automate integration tests using tools like Selenium to simulate user interaction and evaluate the functionality of the system as a whole.

```python
// Selenium test example in Python
from selenium import webdriver

driver = webdriver.Chrome()
driver.get("http://example.com")

# Perform user actions and verify results
```

9.4.2 Continuous Integration and Continuous Delivery (CI/CD)

GitLab CI for Automation: Use CI/CD platforms like GitLab CI to automate building, testing, and deploying code to development, test, and production environments.

```
# GitLab CI configuration
stages:
 - build
```

```
  - test
  - deploy

build:
  script:
    - npm install
    - npm run build

test:
  script:
    - npm test

deploy:
  script:
    - scp ./dist/* user@example.com:/var/www/html/
```

## 9.4.3 Monitoring and Error Management

Implementation of Monitoring Tools: Use tools such as New Relic or Datadog to monitor website performance and availability, identify bottlenecks and proactively respond to issues.

Error Logging and Notification: Set up logging and notification systems to capture and alert about errors in the application. Use services like Sentry orRollbar to centralize error management.

```
// Sentry configuration example in JavaScript
const Sentry = require('@sentry/node');
```

```
Sentry.init({
  dsn: 'YOUR-DSN-GOES-HERE',
  environment: 'production',
});
```

## 9.5 Sustainability and Social Responsibility

Sustainability in web development involves the adoption of practices that minimize environmental impact and promote social responsibility.

### 9.5.1 Resource Optimization

Efficient Energy Use: Optimize code performance to reduce energy consumption, which not only improves efficiency but also contributes to sustainability.

Green Accommodation: Consider choosing accommodation providers that use renewable energy sources and follow sustainable practices.

### 9.5.2 Responsible and Ethical Design
Inclusivity and Diversity: Promote inclusivity and diversity in design and implementation, considering the needs and perspectives of a diverse global audience.

Ethics in Data Collection: Ensure compliance with ethical practices in the collection and use of user data, respecting privacy and confidentiality.

### 9.5.3 Education and Awareness

Continuing Training: Encourage continuing education in sustainability and social responsibility among team members to raise awareness of the implications of development decisions.

Share Best Practices: Engage in the community and share best practices so that the industry as a whole moves towards a more sustainable approach.

9.6 Final Considerations and Future Perspectives

Optimization and the implementation of good practices in web development are essential for creating efficient, secure and accessible websites. The combination of performance strategies, security practices, automated testing, and sustainability considerations lays a solid foundation for modern web development.

As technology advances, we are likely to see new tools and approaches that further improve the efficiency and sustainability of web development. Continued adoption of standards, ethics and sustainability education, and community collaboration are essential to ensuring web development moves forward in a responsible and ethical manner.

In conclusion, optimization and good practices are not only technical aspects of web development, but also a commitment to quality, accessibility and social responsibility. By following these practices and keeping an eye on emerging trends, developers can contribute to a stronger, more sustainable web ecosystem. Let's continue working together to build a better digital future!

# Chapter 10: Advanced Tips and Tricks in Web Development

In the vast and ever-evolving world of web development, advanced tips and tricks can make the difference between standard code and a brilliant, efficient solution. This chapter explores some advanced techniques, best practices, and tricks that can elevate your skills as a web developer and improve the quality and performance of your projects.

## 10.1 JavaScript Code Optimization

Optimizing JavaScript code is essential to ensure agile performance and a smooth user experience. Here, we will explain some advanced strategies to improve the efficiency of your code.

### 10.1.1 Memoization

The Memoization is a technique that allows caching the results of expensive functions to avoid unnecessary calculations. This is especially useful in recursive functions or functions that take a long time to execute.

```javascript
// Example of memoization and JavaScript
const memoize = (func) => {
  const cache = new Map();
  return (...args) => {
    const key = JSON.stringify(args);
    if (!cache.has(key)) {
```

```
    cache.set(key, func(...args));
  }
  return cache.get(key);
 };
};


const expensiveOperation = memoize((n) => {
  console.log(`Executing operation for ${n}`);
  return n * 2;
});


console.log(expensiveOperation(5)); // The operation is
executed and returns 10
console.log(expensiveOperation(5)); // Read from the
cache and return 10 without executing the operation
```

10.1.2 Web Workers

Web Workers are an API that allows scripts to run in the background, without affecting the thread main execution. This is useful for CPU-intensive tasks that could cause UI crashes.

```
// Example of using Web Workers
// In the worker.js file
onmessage = function(e) {
  const result = e.data[0] * e.data[1];
  postMessage(result);
};
```

```
// In the main file
const worker = new Worker('worker.js');
worker.onmessage = function(e) {
  console.log(`Web Worker Results: ${e.data}`);
};
worker.postMessage([5, 2]); // Send data to the Web Worker for processing
```

## 10.1.3 Tree Shaking

Tree shaking is an optimization technique that removes unused code from your bundle. It is commonly used with tools like Webpack and Rollup to reduce the size of the JavaScript file delivered to the browser.

```
// a.js module
export const sum = (a, b) => a + b;
```

```
// Module b.js
export const multiply = (a, b) => a * b;
```

```
// Module main.js
import { sum } from './a';
console.log(sum(2, 3)); // Only the addition function will be included in the final bundle
```

## 10.2 Advanced CSS and Design Techniques

Web design goes beyond the structure of the code. Here, we will explain some advanced CSS techniques to improve the presentation and design of your applications.

## 10.2.1 CSS-in-JS y Styled Components

CSS-in-JS is a technique that allows you to write styles directly in JavaScript. Styled Components is a popular library that implements this technique in React, making it easy to create and manage styles.

```jsx
// Example of Styled Components in React
import styled from 'styled-components';

const StyledButton = styled.button`
  background-color: #4caf50;
  color: white;
  padding: 10px 20px;
  font-size: 16px;
`;

const App = () => {
  return (
    <div>
      <h1>My Application</h1>
      <StyledButton>Click Me</StyledButton>
    </div>
  );
};
```

## 10.2.2 CSS Grid for Complex Layouts

CSS Grid is a powerful tool for creating complex and responsive layouts. It allows the creation of two-dimensional grids that simplify the arrangement of elements.

```css
/* Design example with CSS Grid */
.container {
  display: grid;
  grid-template-columns: repeat(3, 1fr);
  grid-gap: 20px;
}

.item {
  background-color: #3498db;
  color: white;
  padding: 20px;
  text-align: center;
}
```

## 10.2.3 CSS Animations and Transitions

CSS animations and transitions add interactivity and dynamism to your web applications. You can use them to improve the user experience and make your application more attractive.

```css
/* CSS animation example */
@keyframes fadeIn {
  from {
    opacity: 0;
  }
  to {
```

```
  opacity: 1;
 }
}


.fade-in {
  animation: fadeIn 1s ease-in-out;
}
```

10.3 Frontend and Integrated Backend Development

Integrating frontend and backend can simplify development and improve efficiency. Below are some advanced strategies for this integration.

10.3.1 SSR (Server-Side Rendering) con React
Server-Side Rendering is a technique that allows the user interface to be rendered on the server side, improving initial loading speed and indexing by search engines.

```
// SSR configuration example with React and Next.js
// In the pages/index.js file
import React from 'react';


const HomePage = ({ data }) => (
 <div>
   <h1>{data.title}</h1>
   <p>{data.content}</p>
 </div>
);


export async function getServerSideProps() {
```

```
// Logic to get data from the server
const res = await fetch('https://api.example.com/data');
const data = await res.json();


return {
  props: { data },
};
}
export default HomePage;
```

## 10.3.2 GraphQL for Efficient Consultations

GraphQL is a query language that allows clients to request exactly the data they need. This improves query efficiency and reduces data overhead.

```
#Query exampleGraphQL
query {
 user(id: 1) {
   name
   email
   posts {
     title
     content
   }
 }
}
```

## 10.3.3 API Gateways y Microservicios

Using API Gateways and Microservices is an efficient strategy to divide an application into smaller, manageable components. This makes development, scalability and maintenance easier.

```javascript
// API Gateway configuration example with Express.js
const express = require('express');
const app = express();

app.get('/api/data', (req, res) => {
    // Logic to get and consolidate data from multiple microservices
  res.json({ result: 'Consolidated data' });
});

app.listen(3000, () => {
  console.log('API Gateway listening on port 3000');
});
```

10.4 Security in Web Applications

Security is a key priority in web development. Here, we explore some advanced strategies to ensure the security of your applications.

10.4.1 Two-Factor Authentication (2FA)

Two-factor authentication adds an extra layer of security by requiring not only a username and password, but also a second factor, such as a code generated by an app or sent via SMS.

```javascript
// Example of 2FA configuration with Node.js and Passport
const passport = require('passport');
const speakeasy = require('speakeasy');

passport.use(
  new TwoFactorStrategy(
    { usernameField: 'email' },
    async (email, password, done) => {
      const user = await User.findOne({ email });

      if (!user || !user.verifyPassword(password)) {
        return done(null, false, { message: 'Invalid credentials'
});
      }
      if (!user.twoFactorSecret) {
        // User without 2FA setup
        return done(null, user);
      }

      // Generate and send 2FA code
      const token = speakeasy.totp({
        secret: user.twoFactorSecret,
        encoding: 'base32',
      });

      // Send token to the user (for example, via SMS or email)

      // Return information for code validation in the next step
```

```
    return done(null, user, { token });
  }
 )
);
```

## 10.4.2 Protection against Brute Force Attacks

Implement measures to protect against brute force attacks, such as locking accounts after multiple failed attempts or implementing areCAPTCHA on login forms.

```
// Example of brute force protection middleware with Express.js
const rateLimit = require('express-rate-limit');
const limiter = rateLimit({
  windowMs: 15 * 60 * 1000, // 15 minutes
  max: 5, // Maximum number of requests allowed
  message: 'Too many attempts from this IP, please try again
later',
});


app.use('/login', limiter);
```

## 10.4.3 Security Audit and Vulnerability Analysis

Perform regular security audits and vulnerability scans using automated tools and manual code reviews. Identify and address potential security issues proactively.

```
# Example of using security analysis tools in Node.js with npm
audit
npm audit
```

## 10.5 Tools and Development Environment

The development environment and tools you use can have a significant impact on your productivity and code quality. Here, we will explain some advanced tips.

### 10.5.1 Docker for Local Development

Docker makes it easy to create consistent and reproducible local development environments. You can define your environment in a Dockerfile and share it with your team.

```
# Dockerfile example for a Node.js application
FROM node:14

WORKDIR /usr/src/app

COPY package*.json ./

RUN npm install

COPY . .

EXPOSE 3000
CMD ["npm", "start"]
```

### 10.5.2 Pruebas End-to-End con Cypress

Cypress is a powerful tool for end-to-end testing. It allows you to simulate user interaction and evaluate the behavior of the application in a controlled environment.

```
// Test example with Cypress
describe('My Application', () => {
  it('should load the main page', () => {
    cy.visit('/');
    cy.get('h1').should('contain', 'Bienvenido');
  });

  it('you should log in successfully', () => {
    cy.visit('/login');
    cy.get('#username').type('user');
    cy.get('#password').type('contraseña');
    cy.get('form').submit();
    cy.url().should('eq', 'http://localhost:3000/dashboard');
  });
});
```

10.5.3 Use of Alternative Package Managers

Explore alternative package managers like Yarn instead of npm. Yarn offers advantages such as parallel installation of packages and the ability to work offline.

```
# Example of installing packages with Yarn
yarn add package
```

10.6 Ethical and Responsible Development

In addition to technical skills, it is essential to develop in an ethical and responsible manner. Here, we explore some aspects related to ethics in web development.

### 10.6.1 Inclusivity and Diversity
Encourage the inclusivity and diversity in the development team and in product design. Consider different perspectives and experiences to create solutions accessible to all.

### 10.6.2 User Privacy

Respect user privacy and comply with regulations such as the General Data Protection Regulation (GDPR). Clearly communicate data collection and use practices.

### 10.6.3 Environmental Sustainability
Consider environmental sustainability in web development. Opt for practices that reduce energy consumption and minimize environmental impact.

## 10.7 Future Perspectives and Continuous Development

Web development is a constantly evolving field, and the search for continuous improvement is essential. Stay up to date with the latest trends, participate in the community and continue learning to develop more advanced skills.

# Chapter 11: Practical Projects in Web Development

In this chapter, we dive into the exciting world of practical web development projects. Throughout this journey, we explore creating applications from scratch, applying and consolidating the knowledge gained in previous chapters. Through hands-on projects, you will not only build your portfolio, but you will also gain valuable experience and a deeper understanding of how to apply your web development skills in real-world situations.

## 11.1 Project Choice and Initial Planning

Before starting any project, it is crucial to clearly define its purpose and scope. The choice of project should align with your interests and learning goals. Here are some suggestions for practical projects and how you can plan them:

### 11.1.1 Personal Portfolio Project

Purpose: Create a personal website that serves as your portfolio, highlighting your skills, previous projects, and providing information about yourself.

Initial Planning:

Define the Structure: Decide which section you will include, such as a home page, project section, contact information, and possibly a blog.

Design and Style: Choose an attractive design and make sure it reflects your personality and skills.

Technology Selection: Decide what technologies you will use, such as HTML, CSS, possibly a JavaScript framework like React or Vue, and any additional tools for building and deployment.

11.1.2 Task List Application

Purpose: Build a to-do list application that allows users to add, mark as complete, and delete tasks.

Initial Planning:

Basic Functionalities: Lists the main functions, such as adding, editing, marking and deleting tasks.

User Interface (UI): Design a clear and intuitive interface that facilitates task management.

Technologies Used: You can choose to build the app using only HTML, CSS, and JavaScript, or integrate a framework like React for a more dynamic user experience.

11.2 Project Development: Getting to Work

Once you have defined your project and planned the main features, it is time to get to work. Here are some general guidelines for developing practical projects:

11.2.1 Development Environment Configuration

Before you start coding, make sure you have a development environment set up. This may include installing a code editor, setting up version control (such as Git), and establishing a build system if necessary.

```
# Example of installing dependencies with npm (Node.js)
npm install
```

11.2.2 Project Structure and Code Organization

Organizing your project clearly is essential to facilitate development and maintenance. Separate different parts of the project into logical folders and follow naming conventions.

```
/project-practical
  /src
    /components
      Task.js
    /styles
      styles.css
    App.js
    index.js
  /public
    index.html
  README.md
```

11.2.3 Incremental Development and Versioning with Git

Adopting an incremental development methodology allows you to build and test parts of the project step by step. Use Git to version and track changes to your code.

```
# Example of basic Git commands
it's hot
git add .
git commit -m "Project start"
git branch feature-new-functionality
```

11.2.4 Unit and Integration Tests

As you develop, build in tests to ensure your code works properly. Unit tests focus on small parts of the code, while integration tests evaluate how these parts interact.

```
// Example of unit testing with Jest (JavaScript)
test('sum 1 + 2 equals 3', () => {
  expect(summar(1, 2)).toBe(3);
});
```

11.2.5 Responsive Design and Accessibility

If you are building a web application, make sure it is accessible and has a responsive design. Use CSS media queries to adapt the interface to different screen sizes.

```
/* Design exampleresponsive con CSS */
@media screen and (max-width: 600px) {
  /* Styles for small screens */
}
```

## 11.3 Deployment and Optimization

Once you have completed the development of your project, it is time to take it to the web. Here are some key steps for deployment and optimization:

### 11.3.1 Choice of a Hosting Service

Select a hosting service that suits your needs. Platforms such as Netlify, Vercel, GitHub Pages or Heroku offer easy options for deploying web applications.

### 11.3.2 Domain Configuration (Optional)

If you have a custom domain, set up the association with your app. This may involve setting up DNS records or linking your domain to the hosting service.
Host Name: www
Record Type: CNAME
Value: tu-aplicacion.netlify.app

### 11.3.3 Performance Optimization

Before deployment, be sure to optimize your application for optimal performance. This may include file minification, image compression, and the use of caching techniques.

## 11.4 Maintenance and Continuous Improvements

After deployment, your practical project does not end. The maintenance and continuous improvement phase is crucial to ensure that your application remains relevant and functional.

## 11.4.1 Collection of User Comments

Invite real users to use your app and collect their feedback. This can help you identify areas for improvement and fix potential issues that weren't evident during development.

## 11.4.2 Performance Monitoring

Implement performance monitoring tools to stay on top of any issues in real time. This may include loading speed metrics, server response times, and other key performance indicators.

```
// Example of Google Analytics implementation
<script                                                    async
src="https://www.googletagmanager.com/gtag/js?id=GA_MEA
SURE_ID"></script>
<script>
  window.dataLayer = window.dataLayer || [];
  function gtag(){dataLayer.push(arguments);}
  gtag('js', new Date());
  gtag('config', 'GA_MEASURE_ID');
</script>
```

## 11.4.3 Updates and New Features

Listen to user feedback and consider implementing new features or improvements in future versions. Maintain a to-do list and prioritize based on user needs.

11.5 Lessons Learned and Reflections

After completing your hands-on project, reflect on the lessons learned during the process. Consider the following questions:

What challenges did you face and how did you overcome them?
What technologies or approaches did you find most effective?
How could you apply what you learned in future projects?

11.6 Exploring New Horizons

With your practical project completed and valuable experience accumulated, you are in a strong position to explore new horizons in web development. Here are some additional areas you might consider:

11.6.1 Mobile Application Development

Explore mobile app development using technologies like React Native or Flutter. These platforms allow you to build native iOS and Android apps using existing web skills.

11.6.2 Advanced Architectures

Investigate advanced architectures such as microservices, serverless architectures, or event-driven architectures.

These architectures offer scalable and flexible solutions for complex applications.

## 11.6.3 Contributions to Open Source Projects

Consider contributing to open source projects. Participating in development communities gives you the opportunity to work on meaningful projects, collaborate with other developers, and learn from industry experts.

## 11.7 Conclusion: Celebrating Success and Looking to the Future

Congratulations on completing your practical project in web development. This achievement not only demonstrates your ability to apply theoretical concepts, but also highlights your ability to face real-world challenges. With this project as a foundation, you are prepared to take on larger, more complex projects in the future. Continue to learn, experiment and build, the world of web development is full of exciting possibilities!

# Appendix A: Additional Resources on Web Development

In Appendix A, we explore a wide range of additional resources that will complement and enrich your knowledge in the field of web development. These resources range from essential tools and online learning platforms to active communities and key documentation references. Whether you are a beginner taking your first steps or an experienced developer looking to stay up to date, these resources will be very useful.

## A.1 Development Tools and Environments

An efficient web developer requires a set of tools and a development environment that makes it easy to create and maintain projects. Below are some essential tools that can improve your workflow:

### A.1.1 Code Editors

Visual Studio Code (VSCode): A free and open source code editor with a wide range of extensions for different languages and technologies.

Sublime Text: A light and fast editor with a clean and customizable interface.

Atom: Developed by GitHub, Atom is a modern editor, easy to customize and extend.

### A.1.2 Version Control

Git: The most widely used version control system that allows you to track changes to your code and collaborate with other developers.

GitHub: A Git-based platform that facilitates project collaboration, code hosting, and version management.

Bitbucket: Another code hosting platform that provides free private repositories and collaboration tools.

A.1.3 Web Browsers for Development

Google Chrome: With its extensive range of development tools, it is a popular choice for inspecting and debugging code.

Mozilla Firefox Developer Edition: Designed specifically for developers, includes advanced development tools.

Microsoft Edge DevTools: Edge development tools offer a robust experience for debugging and refining your code.

A.1.4 Package Management

npm: The quintessential JavaScript package manager for installation and dependency management.

Yarn: An alternative to npm that offers improvements in speed and consistency in package installation.

A.2 Online Learning Platforms

Continuing education is essential in web development. These online platforms offer courses, tutorials, and resources for all skill levels:

A.2.1 General Platforms

Udacity: Offers courses in collaboration with leading technology companies, focused on industry-specific skills.

Coursera: Provides courses from leading universities and organizations around the world.
edX: Similar to Coursera, edX offers courses in collaboration with renowned academic institutions.

A.2.2 Specialized Platforms in Web Development

freeCodeCamp: A free platform focused on web development that combines interactive learning with hands-on projects.

Codecademy: Offers interactive courses on a variety of web technologies, from HTML and CSS to React and Node.js.

Pluralsight: Specializes in web development courses, providing high-quality content for professional developers.

A.2.3 Tutorials and Documentation

MDN Web Docs: The Mozilla Developer Documentation (MDN) is a comprehensive reference for web technologies, including HTML, CSS, and JavaScript.

W3Schools: An online educational resource to learn web technologies with tutorials and practical examples.

CSS-Tricks: A CSS-focused community offering tutorials, tricks and advanced techniques.

## A.3 Web Development Communities and Forums

Participating in communities and forums is crucial to stay up to date, get help, and connect with other developers. Here are some featured communities:

### A.3.1 Stack Overflow

Stack Overflow: A question and answer platform where developers can ask technical questions and receive answers from the community.

### A.3.2 Communities in Social Networks

Twitter: Follow influential developers, companies, and communities using relevant hashtags like #webdev and #javascript.

Reddit (r/webdev): A subreddit dedicated to web development, where developers share resources, ask questions, and discuss trends.

Dev.to: A community-focused platform for developers sharing articles, tutorials, and experiences.

### A.3.3 Events and Conferences

Meetup: Find local events and web development groups to connect with other developers in person.

Online Conferences: Attend online conferences, such as JSConf, React Summit, and Google I/O, to stay informed on the latest trends and technologies.

A.4 Recommended Books

Books are an invaluable source of knowledge. Here are some recommended books for web developers:

A.4.1 Fundamentals of Web Development

"Eloquent JavaScript" by Marijn Haverbeke: A book that covers the fundamentals of JavaScript and programming.

"HTML and CSS: Design and Build Websites" by Jon Duckett: A visually appealing resource that explores HTML and CSS from scratch.

A.4.2 Advanced and Specialized

"You Don't Know JS" by Kyle Simpson: A series of books that delve into advanced aspects of JavaScript.
"Clean Code: A Handbook of Agile Software Craftsmanship" by Robert C. Martin: An essential book on good coding and software design practices.

A.5 Blogs and Web Development Websites

Explore blogs and websites to stay up to date on the latest news, trends and techniques in web development:

CSS-Tricks: A rich source of tricks, tutorials and articles related to CSS and web design.

Smashing Magazine: Offers in-depth articles on web design, front-end development, and user experience (UX).

A List Apart: Explore topics ranging from HTML and CSS to design and accessibility strategies.

A.6 Open Source Projects

Participating in open source projects is a great way to improve your skills and contribute to the community. Some platforms to find projects are:

GitHub: Explore projects on GitHub and contribute improvements or resolve issues.

Up For Grabs: A website that lists open source projects with friendly tasks for new contributors.

First Contributions: An interactive tutorial to help you make your first contribution to an open source project.

A.7 Certifications and Accreditations

If you're looking to validate your skills, consider earning industry-recognized certifications and accreditations. Some options are:
FreeCodeCamp Certifications: They offer free certifications in complete web development, from design to backend development.

Microsoft Certified: Azure Developer Associate: A certification for developers working with the Microsoft cloud platform.

Google Associate Android Developer Certification: For developers who create applications for the Android platform.

A.8 Podcasts and Multimedia Resources

If you prefer to learn auditorily, podcasts and multimedia resources are excellent options:
Syntax Podcast: A web development podcast covering a variety of topics and technologies.

CodeNewbie Podcast: Designed for beginners, it features interviews with developers from around the world.

Traversy Media (YouTube): A YouTube channel that offers tutorials and practical tips on web development.

A.9 Security and Good Practices

To better understand security in web development and adopt good practices:

OWASP: The Open Application Security Foundation (OWASP) provides resources to improve software security.

Google Web Fundamentals - Security: A guide from Google that addresses secure practices in web development.

A.10 Web Design Resources

If you are interested in web design, these resources will be useful to you:

Dribbble: A website where designers share their work and get inspiration.
Behance: An Adobe platform to showcase and discover creative work, including web design projects.

# Appendix B: Glossary of Terms in Web Development

In Appendix B, we dive into a comprehensive glossary of key terms used in the field of web development. From basic concepts to advanced technologies, this glossary provides clear and concise definitions to help you better understand the language and jargon used in the world of web development.

1. API (Application Programming Interface):

Definition: A set of rules and tools that allows different applications to communicate with each other. APIs define how to interact with a service, library, or component.

2. Backend:

Definition: The part of an application that handles behind-the-scenes operations and server logic. It includes the server, database and application.

3. Database:
Definition: An organized system for storing, managing and retrieving information. It can be SQL (relational) or NoSQL (non-relational), depending on the structure of the data.

4. CDN (Content Delivery Network):

Definition: A system of globally distributed servers that store and serve web content, such as images and files, to improve loading speed.

5. DNS (Domain Name System):

Definition: A system that translates human-readable domain names into IP addresses used by machines on the Internet.

6. DOM (Document Object Model):

Definition: A programming interface that represents HTML and XML documents as tree structures, allowing dynamic manipulation of the page through scripts.

7. Framework:

Definition: A framework or set of tools that provides a foundation for software development. It may include libraries, design patterns, and rules to facilitate development.

8. Git:

Definition: A distributed version control system used to track changes to source code during software development.

9. HTML (Hypertext Markup Language):

Definition: The standard language used to create web pages. Defines the structure and content of a page using tags.

10. IDE (Integrated Development Environment):

- Definition: A set of tools and functions integrated in a single environment to facilitate software development.

11. JavaScript:

- Definition: A high-level programming language that is primarily used to create interactivity in web pages. It is compatible with multiple browsers and platforms.

12. JSON (JavaScript Object Notation):
- Definition: A lightweight data exchange format used to represent structured objects as text. Commonly used in web APIs.

13. LAMP (Linux, Apache, MySQL, PHP/Python/Perl):

- Definition: A technology stack commonly used to develop and host web applications. It includes the Linux operating system, the Apache web server, the MySQL database and a programming language such as PHP, Python or Perl.

14. MVC (Model-View-Controller):

- Definition: A software design pattern that divides an application into three main components: Model (data management), View (presentation) and Controller (business logic).

15. NPM (Node.js Package Manager):

- Definition: A package manager for Node.js that facilitates the installation, management and updating of libraries and tools in projects.

16. REST API (Representational State Transfer):

- Definition: A style of software architecture that uses standard HTTP operations (GET, POST, PUT, DELETE) to perform CRUD operations on resources.

17. SASS (Syntactically Awesome Stylesheets):

- Definition: A CSS preprocessor that extends its functionality by adding features such as variables, nesting and mixins.

18. TDD (Test Driven Development):

- Definition: A development methodology that involves writing tests before writing production code to ensure greater reliability and maintainability.

19. UX/UI (User Experience/User Interface Design):

- Definition: UX refers to the overall user experience when interacting with a product, whileUI she Focuses on visual design and presentation.

20. Virtualization:

- Definition: The creation of a virtual version of resources such as servers, networks or operating systems to optimize efficiency and facilitate development and deployment.

21. WebSocket:

- Definition: A bidirectional communication protocol that allows real-time communication between clients and servers through a persistent connection.

22. XSS (Cross-Site Scripting):

- Definition: A security vulnerability that allows an attacker to inject malicious scripts into web pages visited by other users.

23. YAML (Ain't Markup Language):

- Definition: A human-readable data serialization format commonly used for configuration and structured data.

24. Zeplin:

- Definition: A collaboration tool between designers and developers that facilitates the transfer of designs from design tools to code.

25. 404 Not Found:

- Definition: An HTTP status code indicating that the requested page was not found on the server.
26. 502 Bad Gateway:

- Definition: An HTTP status code that indicates that a server acting as a gateway has received an invalid response.

Glossary Conclusion:
This glossary provides an overview of many key terms in web development. As you advance in your career, this resource will serve as a reference and guide, helping you understand common concepts, technologies, and practices in the exciting world of web development. Stay curious and continue exploring to expand your knowledge in this ever-changing field. Happy developing!

"Dear Reader,

I hope you enjoyed reading 'Simplified CSS3: A Friendly Guide for Beginners'! Your feedback is incredibly valuable to me and other potential readers. If you found the book helpful or enjoyable, would you consider leaving a review on the platform where you purchased it? Your thoughts will not only mean the world to me but will also help others discover and benefit from the book.

Thank you so much for your support!

Best regards,
[DVZ]"



-End-

www.ingramcontent.com/pod-product-compliance
Lightning Source LLC
LaVergne TN
LVHW081531050326
832903LV00025B/1726